Shopping

Contents

What does a newsagent sell?

THE INDEPENDENT
MARSHALL McLUHAN: The message is back
Daily Mail
WIN UP TO £50,000
ILLY PROVED A LAME DUCK WHOSE MEDDLING LOST THE PLAYERS' RESPECT
GOOCH WAS LOOKING FOR SCAPEGOATS AND GOWER PAID THE PRICE
As gardeners face compulsory meters
WATER FIRMS SET FOR RECORD PROFITS
Little boy who has a mother 65 years old
Tories battle to halt election wipeout

What's on TV
Only 47p
LESSONS IN LOVE
THE BEANO
THE U.K.'S No.1 COMIC
EVERY THURSDAY 42p
DENNIS the MENACE and GNASHER

WORDSE
THE UK's BIGGEST
Take a Break's
OVER 60 CODED CROSSWORDS
CODE BREAKERS
Crack our codes for fun and cash!
NEW! ONLY £1.20
GO FOR GOLD! 10 SOVEREIGNS TO BE WON
PLUS £1000 CASH
Up for grabs!

Galaxy
Cadbury's DAIRY MILK
WINE GUMS
FRUIT PASTILLES

What does a toy shop sell?

What does a chemist sell?

HMS MATEY
SAILOR
matey
MILD & GENTLE
NEW
TIMOTEI
with plant milk
MILD SHAMPOO
enriched with herb extracts
NORMAL HAIR
CHILDREN'S
ULTRA
CAVITY
PROTECTION
Great Regular Flavour
Colgate
Total
Colgate

What does a supermarket sell?

tizer
Sunkist
WITH REAL CITRUS

10 JAM & CREAMED BISCUITS
NEW
Jam Splatz

Honey Monster
450 g
Sugar Puffs
24
Weetabix
SAVE UP TO
£50
Jewellery, Watches & Clocks
with THIS pack
Low Sugar Food
Low Fat Food
High Fibre Food

Nimble
WHOLEMEAL
48

Where can you buy these things?

ULTRA CAVITY PROTECTION
Colgate
Colgate
Daily Mail
WIN UP TO £50,000
ILLY PROVED A LAME DUCK WHOSE MEDDLING LOST THE PLAYERS' RESPECT
GOOCH WAS LOOKING FOR SCAPEGOATS AND GOWER PAID THE PRICE
As gardeners face compulsory meters
WATER FIRMS SET FOR RECORD PROFITS
Little boy who has a mother 65 years old
Tories battle to halt election wipeout
MARSHALL McLUHAN:
THE IN
Nimble
WHOLEMEAL
WHOLEMEAL

a b c d e f g h i j k l m n o p q r s t u v w x y z

Index